J
615.109
Tow   Townsend, John

           Pills, powders +
           potions

DUE DATE

A Painful History of Medicine
Pills, Powders + Potions
a history of medication

John Townsend

Chicago, Illinois

For information, address the publisher:
Raintree, 100 N. LaSalle, Suite 1200
Chicago, IL 60602
Customer Service: 888-363-4266
Visit our website at www.raintreelibrary.com

Printed and bound in China by South China
Printing Company
09 08 07 06 05
10 9 8 7 6 5 4 3 2 1

Library of Congess Cataloging-inPublication
Townsend, John, 1955-
  Medication : pills, powders & potions / John
Townsend.
      p. cm. -- (A painful history of medicine)
  Includes bibliographical references and index.
  ISBN 1-4109-1335-X (library bdg.-harcover) --
ISBN 1-4109-1340-6 (pbk.)
1. Drugs--History--Juvenile literature.
2. Pharmacology--History--Juvenile literature.
3. Therapeutics--History--Juvenile literature.
I. Title. II. Series: Townsend, John, 1955-
Painful history of medicine.
  RM301.17.T69 2005
  615'.1'09--dc22
  2004014387

Acknowledgments
Alamy Images pp. **9**, **18–19** (Kathleen
Watmough), **31** (Nigel Cattlin); Art Directors
and Trip p. **26**; A–Z Botanical Collection p. **18**;
Corbis pp. **6** (Keren Su), **7** (Paul A Souders), **10**
(Douglas P Wilson/ Frank Lane Picture Agency),
17 (Stapleton Collection), **24–25** (George D
Lepp), **27**, **28** (Bettmann), **32–33** (Randy Faris),
39 (Mario Beauregard), **43**, **45**, **46**, **48** (D Robert
& Lorri Franz), **48–49** (Craig Lovell), **50**
(Lawrence Manning); Alamy Images/ Dynamic
Graphics Group/ IT Stock Free **p. 42**; Ginny
Stroud-Lewis pp. **4–5**, **23**, **25**, **30–31**, **33**, **38**;
Harcourt Education Ltd/ Tudor Photography p.
36; Mary Evans Picture Library p. **29**; Medical on
Line pp. **10–11**, **16**; Photodisc pp. **50–51**;
Ronald Grant Archive pp. **8–9**; Science Museum/
Science & Society Picture Library pp. **19**, **20**,
20–21, **21**, **28**; Science Photo Library pp. **6–7**
(BSIP, Chassenet), **12–13**, **15**, **23** (Jean-Loup
Charmet), **30** (Andrew Syred), **32** (Th Foto-
Werbung), **34–35** (Joyce Photographics), **35**
(Cordelia Molloy), **37** (Hattie Young), **38–39**
(Edelmann), **40** (Dr P Marazzi), **40–41**
(Professors PM Motta & S Makabe), **41** (Scott
Camazine), **44** (Dept Of Medical Photography, St
Stephen's Hospital, London), **44–45** (John Cole),
47 (CC Studio); The Advertising Archive p. **24**;
The Bridgeman Art Library/ Archives Charmet
p. **6**; The Ronald Grant Archive p. **14**; The
Wellcome Library, London pp. **8**, **22**; ZEFA/
stock4b/ Felbert & Gickenberg p. **13**.

Cover photograph of boy receiving injection
reproduced with permission of Popperfoto
The author and publisher would like to thank
Dr. Justin Miller, D.O. for his assistance in the
preparation of this book.

Every effort has been made to contact copyright
holders of any material reproduced in this book.
Any omissions will be rectified in subsequent
printings if notice is given to the publishers.

The paper used to print this book comes from
sustainable resources.

Contents

Any words appearing in the text in bold,
like this, are explained in the glossary.
You can also look out for them in the "Word
Bank" at the bottom of each page.

Magic Pills

Every hour, people around the world take about 30 million pills! We drink all sorts of powders mixed in glasses of water. We swallow **potions** from millions of bottles. We rub mixtures of all kinds into our skin.

We hope this **medication** will:
- take away pain;
- cure illness;
- stop us from getting sick;
- make us feel good;
- make us look better;
- give us control over our bodies; or
- make us live longer.

If you could make one pill to do all of these things, you would be the richest person alive!

Did you know?

- Most medications today are made in laboratories from mixtures of chemicals.
- Nearly 50 percent of Americans take at least one **prescription drug** each day.
- It often takes twelve years and about $650 million for a new medication to be made and tested before it can be sold.

Most people today have taken some form of medication.

4

Word Bank

medication   substance used to treat illness or disease
medicine   science of dealing with health and disease

Big money

Medical drugs today are big business. Most of us take them at some time to change the way our bodies or minds work.

Thousands of years ago, people found that different foods and plants could affect their health. Different kinds of medication were made from herbs, roots, berries, pods, seeds, bark, leaves, stems, and flowers.

Modern **medicine** still uses chemicals from plants to treat disease. Medication today often works so well because of years of study. But throughout history, this was not always the case.

Find out later . . .

Which pill changed the world of headaches over 100 years ago?

Which Australian tree has been used to make medication for thousands of years?

Which potion uses chopped cockroach to give long life?

potion   liquid mixture that can be used as a medication or poison

Ancient Times

We owe a lot to ancient people. Thousands of years ago, they tried and tested many plants to treat sickness. They would grind up herbs or seeds. Then, they would soak or boil them, sometimes in wine or beer.

The new **medication** then had to be tried. It was often a case of kill or cure.

The Egyptians, then the Greeks and Romans, wrote down which **ingredients** seemed to make different diseases better. They also wrote down which ingredients made things worse.

Dried lizards have been used in traditional Chinese medications.

The first tools of the **medicine** trade.

China

About 4,500 years ago, the Chinese emperor Shen Nung tested hundreds of herbs. He tried out many of them on himself and recorded how they affected him. Some of the barks, roots, and leaves that he tried are still used in **pharmacies** today.

Word Bank   antiseptic   substance that stops harmful bacteria from growing and spreading disease

Egypt

About 4,000 years ago, the Egyptians made all kinds of medications. Many of their ideas, such as using honey as a natural **antiseptic,** worked well.

The Egyptians did not really understand what caused disease. They used magic charms and prayed to gods and spirits when their medication failed.

Opium dissolved in wine was used in all kinds of ways—including to put a noisy child to sleep! In fact, this mixture was still used by some doctors in the 1800s. It was a very dangerous medication, because it is very easy to get **addicted** to opium.

Australia

The **Aborigines** of Australia used leaves from the **eucalyptus** tree to make an ancient **remedy.**

The leaves were crushed and gave off a strong smell. This cleared the nose, throat, and lungs. They were also made into a paste to help heal wounds.

The eucalyptus tree is an important part of Aboriginal medicine.

opium   drug made from opium poppies. It is used to help people relax and to relieve pain.

The Greeks used
the word
pharmakon to
mean **"remedy"** or
"medication." From
this came the word
pharmacy, which
means the
knowledge of
drugs or a place
where drugs are
kept. Pharmacology
is the science of
drugs or medicine.

Kill or cure

The Greek doctor Hippocrates is sometimes
called the father of **medicine.** His ideas have had
a great impact on how we treat illness today.

Hippocrates found how certain drugs acted on
the body. He knew about powerful drugs such
as wine and **opium.** He also knew about deadly
plants such as **mandrake.**

Tiny **doses** of a few poisons can kill some
diseases. But too much can kill the whole body.
The Greeks put a small dose of poisonous
mandrake in wine to help people with **depression.**

A sip of mandrake
would ease the pain
of crucifixion victims.

The root of the
mandrake plant can
be deadly.

Word Bank   crucifixion   put to death by being nailed to
a wooden cross

Mandrake

The root of the mandrake plant can be deadly. It is dangerous to grip it when pulling it from the ground. The Greeks used to pull it up with ropes to avoid getting the poison on their hands.

The Romans made mandrake into a "death wine" and dipped sponges into it. They would offer them on a stick to **crucifixion** victims. The **potion** put them in a deathlike sleep and eased their suffering until they died.

Bald

People have always rubbed things on their heads to cure baldness.

- Hippocrates treated baldness with pigeon droppings.
- The Greek teacher Aristotle tried using goat's **urine** on his own head.
- The Roman emperor Julius Caesar used a paste made of ground horse teeth and deer **marrow.**

Cures for baldness don't tend to work!

dose   amount or measure of a medication or drug
mandrake   poisonous plant. The root was once used as a drug.

A Saint John's Wort plant.

Romans

By 200 BC the Romans had taken over many countries. For the next 400 years, they ruled large areas around the **Mediterranean Sea.**

Their cities had many healers who sold all kinds of **medications.** They were not only doctors, but also school teachers and so-called "wise women."

The Romans used all kinds of **ointments** to clean wounds and **ulcers.** One of these was made from a deadly poison. It was **arsenic.** This white powder has been useful to doctors—as well as poisoners—for years.

Healing plants

Some of the medications found at old Roman sites include dock leaves, which were used to treat bad teeth and stiff legs.

A plant called Saint John's Wort has also been found at the remains of Roman villages. It is used today for sore skin and **depression.**

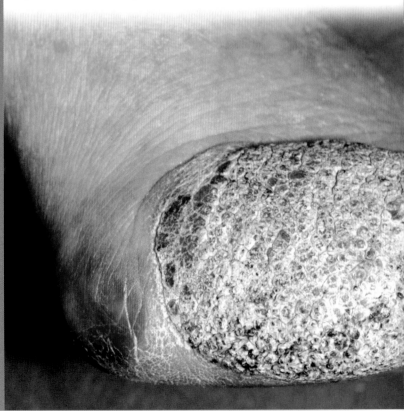

Word Bank   **licorice**   plant root that is used in many medications and in cooking

Galen

Galen was a famous doctor in Rome in the year AD 160. He used all kinds of mixtures to treat patients. One had 77 **ingredients** in it, including the flesh of snakes. These were mixed with honey and rubbed on the teeth and gums. This mixture was thought to cure most problems, including snake bites.

Fast facts

An ancient cure for warts was to rub on "ashes of white dog's dirt and oil of roses." More often than not, the cure was worse than the problem it was supposed to treat!

People wrongly believed warts were caught from toads!

Soldiers

Roman soldiers often had to march 30 miles (50 kilometers) a day. They were given a daily **dose** of **licorice** to stop them from getting thirsty.

Garlic was rubbed onto battle wounds to heal them. This was smelly but effective, because garlic juice is a **disinfectant**.

ointment   oily substance rubbed onto skin for medicinal reasons
ulcer   open sore, often full of pus

The Middle Ages

Moving on

Medical knowledge from Rome and Greece was taken to Islamic countries. Here, plants grew that could not be found anywhere else in the world. From the 8th century AD, Muslims added new plants to their wide range of drugs. Some of these were rhubarb, nutmeg, and cloves.

The **Middle Ages** were a time of new ideas about **medicine**, especially in **Islamic** countries. **Islam,** the religion followed by Muslims, teaches people how to care for the body.

The main city of the Islamic world was Baghdad. By the Middle Ages it was a very rich city, with over one million people.

A **pharmacy** in Baghdad made and sold many new **medications.** Some of them had over 100 **ingredients.** At the time, Islamic medicine was the most advanced in the world.

An Arab doctor makes a medication to treat snake bites.

Word Bank   **Islam**   religion of Muslims, who follow the teaching of the prophet Muhammad

Islamic medicine

Islamic doctors developed the medical ideas begun by the Romans and Greeks. They also invented new drugs, using herbs in many different ways.

They boiled plants in water to collect the steam. Patients inhaled (breathed in) the steam to ease breathing problems. If a **remedy** worked, it would be written down, and so the knowledge could be passed on.

Islamic medicine is important in our understanding of many drugs today. In fact, words such as *drug, alcohol,* and *syrup* all came from the Islamic world in the Middle Ages.

Yuk!

Islamic doctors tried to change the idea that the more horrible medication tasted, the better it was for you! They used flavorings made of rose water and orange-blossom water.

But not all of their medication tasted nice. One was made of leaves boiled in camel **urine**. Yuk!

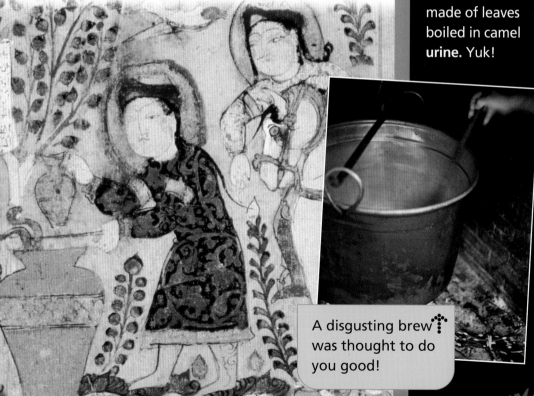

A disgusting brew was thought to do you good!

Middle Ages   period of history roughly between AD 500 and AD 1500

13

Monks

It was not just the **Islamic** faith that grew during the **Middle Ages.** The **Christian** Church spread across much of Europe.

The church built many **monasteries,** where **monks** lived, studied, and took care of the sick. They often grew herbs in monastery gardens. They also gathered plants from nearby woodlands and fields.

Monks who traveled to other countries returned home with new plants. These would be boiled and their juices tested on patients. If they worked, the recipe would be written down.

Monks made medications for all kinds of sicknesses.

Word Bank   **Christian**   follower of Jesus Christ and the religion based on his teachings

Worth a try

The treatments made by monks in the Middle Ages were not all a matter of guesswork. They tried to make links between certain plants and illnesses:

The leaves of lungwort look like lungs, so use them for chest infections.

A walnut looks like the brain, so use it to cure headaches.

Use yellow plants to cure diseases that make the skin yellow, such as **jaundice**.

But none of these treatments really worked. It was time to be a little more scientific.

Not much good

Monks did their best to find a cure for the dreaded **plagues** that swept across Europe in the Middle Ages.

The **pope's** doctor mixed butter with figs and onions to put on swellings caused by the plague.

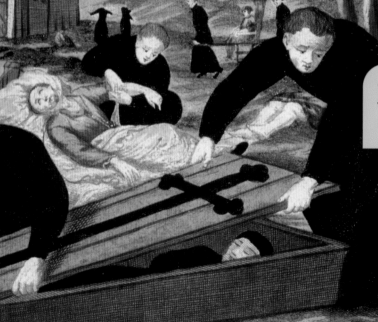

Caring for plague victims in the Middle Ages.

monk   member of a religious community of men
plague   deadly disease that spreads quickly

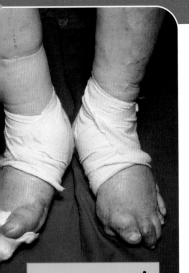

Gout is a painful swelling of the foot.

Doctors and drug stores

Where would you go if you felt sick in the **Middle Ages**? Many villages had a "wise woman," or witch, who used **potions** to treat illness. Her **medications** would be made of local plants, spices, and stones. These were used in drinks, pills, baths, rubs, **poultices,** and bandages.

If you did not want a witch to treat you, you could pay to see a trained doctor, a **monk,** or a **midwife.** Many towns also had their own **pharmacy,** run by someone called an **apothecary.**

Swollen foot

"Cut off the hind legs of a frog and wrap them in deer skin. Put the frog's right leg on the right foot and the left leg on the left foot of the patient. He will soon be cured."

*A cure for **gout** from a doctor in the 11th century*

An apothecary at work in his shop in 1751.

Word Bank   apothecary   maker and keeper of drugs
gout   painful swelling of the toe

Mixtures

Drug stores in the 1200s had shelves lined with jars, bottles, and **mortars.** All pills, powders, potions, and pastes were made by hand. Pills were rolled between the palms of the apothecary's hands, which were often rubbed in almond oil. The pills were then left to dry and harden.

Molasses was said to stop swellings, cure **fevers,** unblock the stomach, help people sleep, heal wounds, and cure the **plague.** In fact, it probably just tasted nice and that was all!

Pharmacists and pharmacies developed from early apothecary shops.

mortar   pot in which material is pounded with a tool called a pestle
poultice   soft, heated bag or bandage put onto a sore

Good for Business

Selling poison

French **pharmacists** began to study the effects of poisonous plants. They made **strychnine** from the seeds of the dog button plant from India. This deadly poison can cause painful death. But in very tiny **doses,** it was used to improve the appetite after illness.

Sick people will often pay any amount of money to feel better. The problem for patients is knowing whether or not they are spending their money wisely.

Trial and error

There was a lot of trial and error with **medications** in the 1600s and 1700s. Some doctors used their patients as guinea pigs to try out new mixtures. It was always hit and miss as to whether they worked.

Some **remedies** were horrible. They used oil from earthworms, spiders' webs, human fat, woodlice, and crushed pearls. What a disgusting mixture!

Strychnine comes from the deadly dog button plant.

Word Bank

kidney stone   hard lump that builds up in the kidney
rectum   opening from the bowel to the anus

Tobacco

In 1774 a **tobacco** blower was invented to bring a dead body back to life! It blew tobacco smoke into the patient's **rectum,** nose, or mouth.

But no one realized how dangerous tobacco was. One Spanish doctor named Nicolas Monardes used it to treat toothaches, bad breath, worms, joint pains, cold swellings, and **kidney stones.** Chewing tobacco was even thought to protect people against the **plague.**

John Bell's pharmacy in London.

Open all hours

In 1798 John Bell opened a high-class **pharmacy** in London. He sold pills, powders, and **potions** to rich customers. The shop opened at 7 A.M. and did not close until 11 P.M. It was a very successful business.

Tobacco leaves were once thought to help cure diseases!

strychnine kind of poisonous powder
tobacco dried leaves of a plant used for smoking or chewing

Quack doctors

At one time anyone could be a doctor. If you had a few mixtures to sell to sick people, you were in business. Many had a basic knowledge of **medicine,** but some were just cheats.

In the 1700s there was a rise in the number of these "quack" doctors. They went from village to village selling worthless **medications.** There were still so many different ideas about what caused sickness that people believed the quacks. Sick people were so desperate they would try anything.

Quack doctors talked quickly to fool people into buying their goods.

Did you know?

The word *quack* comes from *quacksalver.* This was someone who sold **salves** and other healing **remedies.**

Word Bank   remedy   medication or treatment that is meant to make an illness better

Electrifying

Quack doctors could claim their pills and **potions** did anything. There was no law to stop them from telling lies. Some even said their mixtures stopped people from getting old.

In 1779 James Graham opened his Temple of Health in London. He charged a lot of money for people to go inside for treatment. Some customers paid to be washed in mud. Graham said this would give them a long life. Some paid to sleep in an electrified bed to get rid of their problems. It just got rid of their money!

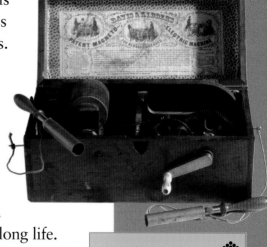

An electrical machine that was said to cure any illness.

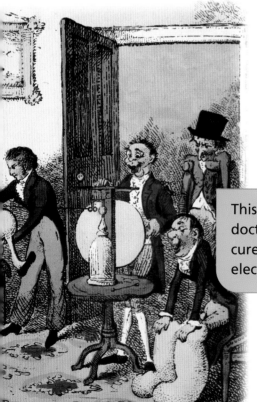

This quack doctor is trying to cure a patient by electrifying her!

End of the quacks

Quack doctors disappeared when real **pharmacies** opened in most towns. By the 1800s laws stopped them from selling their false medications. Even so, medications that made all kinds of false claims were still available well into the 1900s.

salve   healing or soothing ointment

Success story

A common disease during the 1700s was **edema.** This caused water to fill parts of the body, making people swell up like a balloon. Their lungs got crushed, and they could no longer breathe.

In 1775 a British doctor, William Withering, could not help a patient dying from edema. But the patient got a **remedy** from a gypsy. In a few days he was better. Withering hunted down the gypsy and begged her to tell him what was in this magic **potion.** She told him the main **ingredient** was a foxglove flower.

Life and death

The drug digitalis became important in 1775. It is still used to treat some heart conditions.

But digitalis can also kill people. It causes severe sickness and **diarrhea.** Because it is deadly, digitalis is often used in rat poison.

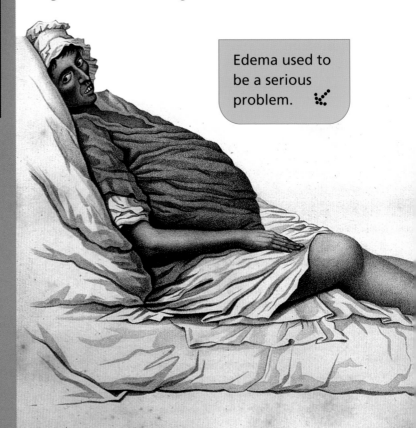

Edema used to be a serious problem.

Word Bank   edema   illness causing fluid collection in the body. It often resulted in death.

Heart disease

Withering knew that the foxglove contained a chemical called **digitalis,** which could be deadly. Even so, he tried out digitalis on 158 of his patients.

Withering had always wondered whether there was a link between edema and heart disease. Giving his heart patients dried foxglove leaves seemed to help their hearts and cure their edema.

Edema, the swollen man, is shown with tuberculosis, the withered woman.

This was a major discovery. Digitalis brought an end to the misery of edema as well as to some kinds of heart disease.

The foxglove plant can kill and cure. It contains digitalis.

Fat and thin

Two of the dreaded diseases of the 1700s had very different effects on patients. Edema made victims swell up to a very large size. **Tuberculosis** made victims weak and thin.

By the end of the century, there was a cure for edema. The cure for tuberculosis took much longer.

tuberculosis   disease that causes fever and lung failure

Mixtures from the 1800s

During the 1800s, people began to travel more widely. They came across all sorts of different treatments on their travels.

Old home remedies

Most homemade **remedies** used **ingredients** from the kitchen, such as:

- beetroot to give strength;
- hot water and pepper for an upset stomach; and
- bread **poultice** for a sore throat.

> "Cover snails in brown sugar and wrap them in a clean cloth. Hang the cloth over a basin and let the juice drip into it. Drink the liquid."

An old British cure for a sore throat

Brown sugar and snail slime—just right for a sore throat!

Punishment

Many people in the 1800s kept a bottle of castor oil in the cupboard. The oil tasted horrible and was often given to children as a punishment. It was also a strong **laxative,** so it was a good idea to behave!

Word Bank   asthma   disease affecting the lungs that makes breathing difficult

United States

In isolated parts of the United States, there were few doctors. Most mothers made a supply of home **medications** for their families:

For a chest cold, spread on goose grease.
For a chest pain, put on a hot cloth covered with sheep fat.
For sprained joints, mix apple vinegar with the white of one egg.

Some **Native American** tribes chewed a nasty-smelling plant called skunk cabbage to ease **asthma.** Scientists today think this probably would have worked.

Oozing

An old woman from Maryland who was born in the 1800s had a cure for **athlete's foot:**

" Find a fresh cow pie and, while it is still smoking-hot, stick your sick foot in it for a while. "

Worth a try?

Some people thought standing in a fresh cow pie could cure disease.

In the wars

The United States **Civil War** started in 1861. The North and the South began to fight each other because they disagreed about slavery and how to run the country. The battles left thousands of soldiers badly hurt.

There was never enough **medication** to go around the **field hospitals.** Many of the doctors had to make do with plants they found nearby.

One doctor said:

"I made **laxatives** from peach-tree leaves boiled into a strong tea. I even gave the men heated lard mixed with syrup.**"**

Progress

Wars in the 1800s actually helped to improve **medicine.** Caring for so many sick and injured people made doctors try new remedies and find out more about how drugs worked.

The U.S. Civil War taught doctors a lot about medicine.

Word Bank   civil war   when soldiers from the same country fight against one another

Treating wounds

A big problem during the civil war was gunshot wounds. These often got badly **infected** and **gangrene** set in. To stop gangrene from spreading, doctors cut off patients' arms and legs. But often the gangrene returned to the stump—unless medication was found to treat the **infections**.

❝ Out of a hundred operations to remove infected limbs, twenty or thirty are doing well. This is because we use medications such as **quinine**. Otherwise, we use **remedies** we can get from the woods. ❞

Surgeon Joseph Jones

Powerful mixture

Many civil war soldiers had **bowel** problems caused by poor living conditions.

In one Tennessee unit, Dr. Cowan gave patients **Epsom salts, bicarbonate of soda,** and **opium** powder dissolved in water. This treatment worked so well that the doctor was soon promoted to major!

A nurse cares for wounded soldiers in the U.S. Civil War.

gangrene   when flesh rots and dies due to infection or lack of blood supply

Big business

Lydia Pinkham was a housewife from Massachusetts. In 1873 she began to sell a **medication** that she had been making for her family for years. She put her own portrait on the box (below) and called it "Lydia E. Pinkham's Vegetable Compound." It contained herbs and alcohol. She claimed it cured cramps and stopped women from getting dizzy when wearing corsets (tight undergarments).

When Lydia died in 1883, her mixture was earning her $300,000 a year. In 1925 it made $3.8 million!

Medicine jokes

Cartoons in the 1800s made fun of the latest in **medicine.** The one above is from 1834 and shows the "Extraordinary Effects of Morrison's Vegetable Pills."

It shows how the man on the left can now walk after taking his pill. He woke up to find he had grown a new pair of legs. Of course, this was impossible!

LYDIA E. PINKHAM'S

VEGETABLE COMPOUND

Word Bank **immune** protected from catching a disease
stress feeling under too much pressure

Snake-oil salesman

In the 1880s John Meyer, a salesman from Nebraska, traveled around by wagon. When **Native Americans** told him about the healing powers of a type of root, he made it into a juice. He sold it in bottles, claiming it could cure cancer, mad-dog bites, and even the **plague.** Meyer even let rattlesnakes bite him to prove his cure stopped him from getting sick!

The root he used was echinacea. Some people believe it boosts the **immune** system.

Can you believe it?

Some medications claimed to do amazing things:
- Dr. Gordon's Elegant Pills were supposed to make you slim.
- Clarke's Blood Mixture was for skin disorders, swellings, and **gout.**
- Dr. Cassell's Nerve Tablets were for sleeplessness and **stress.**
- Dr. Williams' Pink Pills claimed to strengthen the blood after illness.

In the 1870s, Wind Pills claimed to cure "wind of the stomach" and "all complaints of the **bowels** or liver."

Worms

Some types of worm can live inside our bodies. When tapeworms lay eggs, these pass out of our bodies in **excrement**. The eggs then go into the soil and are eaten by animals. If humans eat meat from these animals, the eggs may get inside us. The worm grows and the cycle starts again.

As the tapeworm grows, it eats food that enters the stomach. The record length for a tapeworm in a human is 108 feet (33 meters). Some people have even swallowed tapeworm eggs on purpose to lose weight!

Did you know?

Tapeworms can live in our **intestines.** They take in **nutrients** from our food and can keep growing for years. Most tapeworm **infections** come from our food and water.

Undercooked meat is one source. Our pets may also pass eggs from their fur to our hands, nose, and mouth.

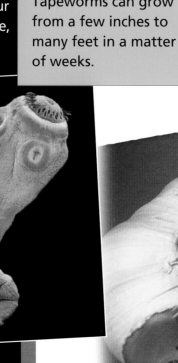

Tapeworms can grow from a few inches to many feet in a matter of weeks.

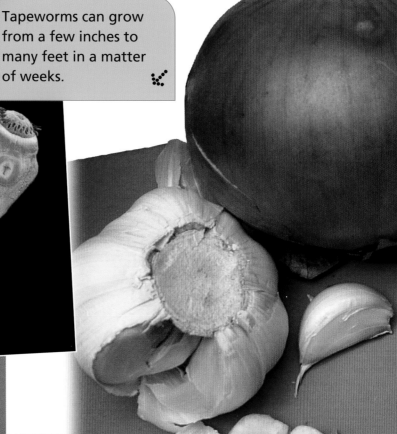

Word Bank

intestine   part of the body that goes from the stomach to the anus. It is where food is digested.

Garlic

Having worms can make you sick. One old treatment was to starve the patient for three days. This would also starve the worms. Then, hot soup was held at the patient's mouth. People thought the worms would come up the throat to feed on the soup. Someone would wait to grab the worm as it poked out of the patient's mouth. This never worked!

Eating onions and garlic was a better way to get rid of worms. Modern drugs can now deal with the problem.

Cockroaches were used as medication!

Garlic and onions have always been seen as good for health—but not so good for nice breath!

Cockroach pills

In some Asian countries, people believe cockroaches can cure sicknesses. Many people are convinced they help fight colds. Some people even think that eating cockroaches will make them live longer!

Wonder Drugs

Some drugs have had a great impact on the health of millions of people.

Acid

For hundreds of years, people living near willow trees found that chewing white willow bark could ease pain.

In England in 1758, Edward Stone chewed some white willow bark to see if it helped his **fever** and toothache.

He was so impressed with the result that he wrote to some scientists about it. They found that an acid in the bark was a good painkiller. This discovery would change the world.

Tea made from the white willow bark was used to treat fevers.

Word Bank   fever   very high body temperature caused by illness
heart attack   sudden failure of the heart

Aspirin

Scientists began to study the acid and its effects. The problem was how to turn the white willow bark into a drug that did not irritate the mouth and stomach.

In 1897 a German scientist named Felix Hoffmann made a chemical based on the acid. He called it acetylsalicylic acid (ASA).

By 1899 the Bayer drug company gave ASA its brand name: Aspirin. At first it was only sold to doctors and hospitals as a powder. In 1915 it was made into tablet form.

Aspirin can be swallowed whole or dissolved in water.

Lifesaver

Aspirin is a painkiller. It is also used to help prevent **heart attacks** and **strokes.** Aspirin probably saves more than 100,000 lives each year by preventing heart disease.

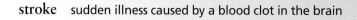

stroke   sudden illness caused by a blood clot in the brain

Penicillin

A great discovery in the 1900s was an **antibiotic** drug called **penicillin.** In 1928 a British scientist named Alexander Fleming found penicillin growing on a dish of **bacteria.** He saw how it destroyed the bacteria.

It took another twelve years for Fleming and other scientists to test it and make it into a drug. They were amazed at how penicillin helped the body fight disease.

From the 1940s the new drug was used around the world.

Penicillin tablets have been lifesavers.

Word Bank   antibiotic   substance that kills harmful bacteria

Early days

Until the 1940s people often died if their wounds got **infected** and poisoned their blood. Penicillin was able to stop this from happening.

The problem for scientists in the 1930s was how to grow enough penicillin to use on patients. They grew it in milk churns, bottles, and bedpans.

One patient was a policeman dying of blood poisoning. Scientists gave him all the penicillin they had, and he began to get better. But after four days, the penicillin ran out and the policeman died.

Scientists eventually figured out how to make larger amounts of penicillin.

Superbugs

Antibiotics have helped save millions of lives—but there is one problem. Some bacteria are becoming **resistant** to them. These bacteria multiply to make superbugs that antibiotics cannot kill. Scientists then have to make new antibiotics to try to kill the new superbugs!

Penicillin mold growing on a tangerine.

bacteria   tiny group of living things. Some can cause disease
penicillin   first type of antibiotic

Mystery disease

For years the disease **diabetes** puzzled doctors. People with diabetes could eat and drink a lot and still lose weight. They felt tired, got stomach pains, and had skin and eye problems. Eventually, the disease would kill them. The problem was their bodies were losing sugar in their **urine.**

So, how could doctors tell if a patient had diabetes? Simple. They sipped his or her urine. If the urine was very sweet, the patient had diabetes. The trouble was, not much could be done to treat the disease.

Sweet urine is a sign of diabetes.

Word Bank

diabetes   disease in which the body is unable to use sugars in the way it needs to for everyday function

Breakthrough

The greatest discovery in the treatment of diabetes came in 1921. Two scientists in Canada experimented on a dog. Frederick Banting and Charles Best removed the dog's **pancreas** so it could not make **insulin.**

This gave the dog diabetes. They then injected it with another dog's insulin. This controlled the sugar levels in the diabetic dog.

Scientists then took insulin from pigs to inject into humans with diabetes. This was a major breakthrough. It meant that at last people with diabetes were able to control their disease.

Big difference

About 17 million people in the United States and 100 million people around the world have diabetes today. Since the 1980s, new ways of making and injecting insulin have been developed to help people with diabetes lead normal lives.

A special pen clicks an amount of insulin, so anyone can easily get the right **dose.**

pancreas   organ near the stomach that controls sugar in the blood

Modern Times

In the last 50 years, some amazing new **medications** have been developed. Progress is only possible because of years of tests and hard work by scientists.

Drugs disaster

Not all drugs have been successful. A drug called Thalidomide first came out in 1956. It helped women who felt sick while they were pregnant. But the drug was not tested properly, and it did serious damage to unborn babies. Many babies were born with arms and legs missing.

Danger

Drugs always carry risks. Chemicals can react badly inside us. Some people have an **allergy** to certain drugs. Some drugs react badly if taken with other substances. Any medication must be used carefully.

An unborn baby inside the womb at seven weeks.

Word Bank   **disabled**   having a physical or mental problem that can affect everyday life

Risk

For five years, Thalidomide was used in many countries. The United States delayed using it until more tests had been done. Taking even a single **dose** seemed to cause harm.

In 1962 the drug was banned. But by then 12,000 **disabled** children had been born in the United Kingdom, Europe, Australia, Canada, and Japan.

Thalidomide is now being used again, but not by pregnant women. The drug can treat skin problems of people with **leprosy**, AIDS (see page 44), and some types of cancer. It has to be taken very carefully.

Big question

The Thalidomide tragedy resulted in all new drugs being tested far more carefully. This can sometimes mean testing them on animals before trying them on people.

Some people think it is wrong to use animals for testing drugs. What do you think?

Cancer drugs

Cancer is a disease that many people fear today. It develops when body **cells** begin to grow out of control. These abnormal (not normal) cells often form a **tumor.** They can also spread to other parts of the body. Some cancers affect the blood.

In the last 50 years, great progress has been made in treating some types of cancer. Important new chemicals have been discovered in plants. The bark of the Pacific yew tree is used to make an anticancer drug called paclitaxel. Since 1992 this drug has saved the lives of many women with cancer of the **ovaries.**

Too much sunbathing is known to cause skin cancer.

The battle goes on

For hundreds of years, doctors have tried to fight the different forms of cancer. It is still a serious illness, but there have been many successes in the last few years. The death rate from cancer is gradually going down.

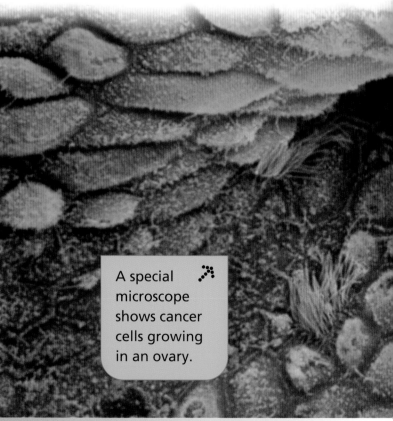

A special microscope shows cancer cells growing in an ovary.

Word Bank

cell   tiny building blocks that make up all living things
ovary   female organ that produces eggs

Hope

By the year 2000, scientists needed to develop a new drug to replace paclitaxel. Each patient needed six whole 100-year-old trees for their drugs, and the trees were quickly running out.

Scientists found it was possible to use chemicals from other types of yew tree.

In 2004 a drug called bevacizumab was found to stop blood from getting to cancer cells. This stops tumors from growing out of control for a while. Although it does not cure cancer, bevacizumab can give patients extra months or even years of life.

Rainforests

The Madagascan periwinkle (below) is a rainforest plant containing over 70 chemicals. Two of these chemicals can kill cancer cells in the blood. Many other rainforest plants may contain cancer cures.

tumor   unusual growth in the body

Treating the mind

One health problem that affects millions of people around the world is **depression.** For those who suffer badly from this illness, life can be miserable.

Depression affects people's thoughts, moods, feelings, and behavior. In the past, patients were just told to "snap out of it."

Today, doctors know that depression is much more than a case of "the blues." Chemicals in the brain can sometimes get out of balance and cause problems.

Great progress has been made in understanding how these chemicals work and how they can affect us.

Exercise can be good for the mind as well as the body.

42

antidepressant   drug to treat depression
depression feeling very down, upset, and deeply unhappy

Pill-popping

Many "mind drugs" came out in the second half of the 1900s.

- 1950s: Lithium was the first drug to help control mood swings and depression.
- 1960s: Librium was a new **tranquilizer.** It became the world's most popular **prescription drug.**
- 1963: Valium was first given to help **stress.** Many people became **addicted** to this drug.
- 1987: Prozac was a new **antidepressant.** By 2000, 40 million people in 100 countries had taken Prozac.

Bananas

Eating a banana can cheer you up. Bananas are the only fruit to contain a special **ingredient** that helps the body produce serotonin. That is why bananas are often called "good mood food."

Some drugs boost the amount of serotonin in the brain to help treat depression.

serotonin   chemical in the brain that helps the "feel good" factor
tranquilizer   drug to help calm and relax

HIV and AIDS

In the early 1980s, doctors were trying to deal with a new disease. A **virus** seemed to be spreading, which they called the Human Immunodeficiency Virus (HIV). It was passed from person to person through bodily fluids.

HIV could develop into a condition called AIDS (Acquired **Immune** Deficiency Syndrome). People with AIDS are unable to fight **infections.**

AIDS is now a major worldwide **epidemic.** For 25 years scientists have studied the illness. They have made a lot of progress, but there still is no cure.

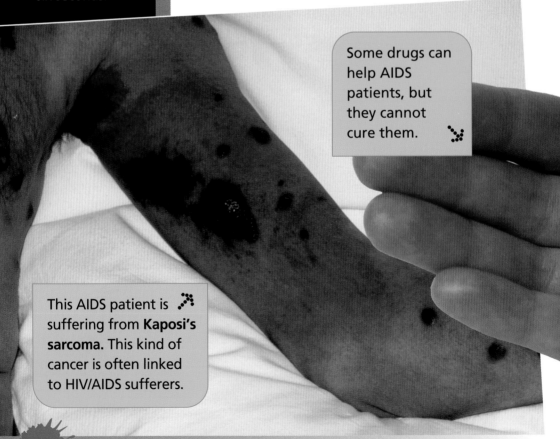

Some drugs can help AIDS patients, but they cannot cure them.

This AIDS patient is suffering from **Kaposi's sarcoma.** This kind of cancer is often linked to HIV/AIDS sufferers.

Word Bank   epidemic   outbreak of a disease that spreads quickly over a wide area

The search continues

Some drugs can slow down the effects of AIDS. But almost half the patients who try the drugs do not get better.

Most AIDS drugs help to stop new viruses from getting into the body. But the drugs can have side effects such as **kidney stones,** blurred vision, headaches, and rashes.

One new drug called Reverset has fewer of these side effects. It can be taken as a pill each day and offers hope to some patients. Other new drugs are being developed and tested.

The AIDS symbol is now known all over the world.

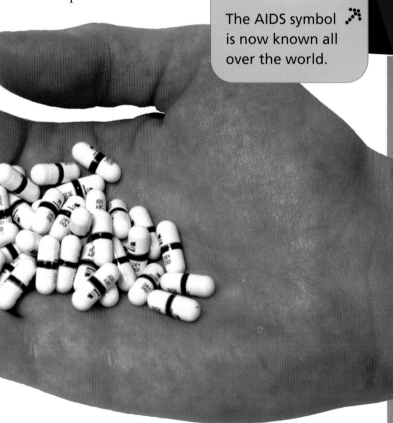

Major problem

Drug treatment for AIDS in the United States costs over $10,000 per patient per year. This is far too much money for people in poor countries.

There are 42 million people worldwide with HIV, and 95 percent of these live in poor countries.

virus tiny living thing that breaks into the body's cells and can cause disease

One hundred years ago, doctors had to manage with only a few drugs. One of them contained **opium** to kill pain, just as the Egyptians used 4,000 years before.

The choice of drugs has never been greater than it is today.

Big changes

Drugs were once just swallowed as pills, powders, or **potions.** Today, they can get into the body with a shot, a patch, or a puff.

- A shot from a **vaccine** gun was used for a disease called **smallpox** in the 1960s.
- Skin patches can now be stuck onto the body to pass drugs slowly into the bloodstream.
- With a quick "puff" on an **inhaler, asthma** sufferers can breathe a fine mist into their lungs. This widens the airways and helps their breathing.

Pills are made in the millions in factories such as this.

Word Bank   inhaler   device for breathing in a drug
smallpox   disease causing blisters all over the body

Drugs in the United States

Medical drugs are bigger business now than ever before.

- **Prescription drugs** are given well over three billion times a year in the United States.
- Drug companies spend over $3 billion a year to advertise drugs.
- Each year, 8.5 million Americans buy drugs as a result of these advertisements.

Even though there are hundreds of **medications** around today, some people prefer not to take them at all. They are returning to the natural drugs found in plants. Many companies are now producing drugs made from plant extracts.

Too much choice?

Now that supermarkets are open all day and e-**pharmacies** offer medications online, dealing with a headache has never been easier. For example, there are over fifteen different types of aspirin to choose from. The headache is deciding which kind to use!

A vaccine gun fires a quick **dose** into the arm of this patient.

vaccine   medication to make the body defend itself against a disease

In the news

Medicine makes big news today. Here are some of the stories from 2004:

VICTIM LOSES SKIN

A Californian woman lost all her skin after a bad reaction to an **antibiotic.** Sarah Yeargain watched in terror as her skin peeled away. Doctors thought she would die.

Even the skin in her mouth, throat, and eyes fell off. Doctors covered her entire body with a new man-made skin. They also gave her drugs to stop the bleeding.

Her own skin has now started to grow back. Her recovery is being called a medical miracle.

Testing drugs on baboons may help to treat humans with **obesity.**

Beat obesity

Scientists in Texas have found a drug that makes overweight mice thin and healthy. They believe the treatment could work on humans.

Mice lost 30 percent of their body weight in just four weeks. The next tests will be on baboons, which gain weight in the same way as humans.

Word Bank   obesity   being very overweight

The best medicine is changing address!

Eight-year-old Luis Manon lived in Cuzco, Peru, which is 11,024 feet (3,360 meters) above sea level. There is less oxygen in the air at this height, and Luis had an undeveloped heart which needed more oxygen. His illness made him tired and very weak. Doctors said he needed an expensive operation, which his parents could not afford. Instead, they moved to Brazil where their new home was much closer to sea level and there was more oxygen in the air.

Days after moving to Rio de Janeiro, in Brazil, Luis felt fine. All he needed was a change of address, not heart surgery or drugs.

Licorice

Scientists in Edinburgh, Scotland, think a drug found in **licorice** could improve the memory. They have been testing it on older people with memory problems.

So far the drug has helped them remember things far better. They just have to remember to take it!

Cuzco in the mountains of Peru.

And finally . . .

Even in the 21st century, some amazing medical claims are made.

Would you believe it?

In 2004 the makers of special tights sold in Austria said they helped women lose weight. This new product soon sold out.

Dr. Wurgler from Vienna, Austria, said the tights have **caffeine** in them, which helps to break down fat:

"The results are amazing. Once inside the body, the caffeine stimulates the burning of fat and the effects are soon seen."

These claims have yet to be proven!

Laughter is the best medicine.

Laughter: The Best Medicine

Patients suffering from **depression, stress,** and **diabetes** in Brazil are being given "laughter classes." They all have to laugh out loud together. The staff organizes activities to make patients giggle. Dr. Sales said, "A good laugh can help to treat many conditions."

Word Bank

acne   skin condition causing red spots, usually on the face
caffeine   drug found in coffee and tea

The future

For thousands of years, we have taken pills, powders, and **potions** to cure sickness, make us feel or look good, and make us live longer. We still dream of finding that magic **medication** that solves all our problems.

With today's research, it may only be a matter of time before more amazing treatments are available.

We may find cures for AIDS and cancer. Medication may one day cure everything from baldness to **obesity.** A simple pill may stop us from aging. We could all look young and live forever.

Medical myths

As we keep learning more about **medicine,** perhaps **myths** such as these will one day be a thing of the past:

Junk food gives you pimples. FALSE

Acne is caused by dead skin **cells,** hormones, and **bacteria.**

If you do not wear warm clothes, you will catch a cold. FALSE

Viruses are the only cause of colds.

How do you feel about being able to live forever?

myth   made-up tale that is told over the years and passed on

Find Out More

Did you know?

- The world's largest sculpture made of flowers was built to look like a strip of aspirin tablets! It took one week for 1,914 people in Jakarta, Indonesia, to complete the sculpture in 1999.

- The leech is the best animal to bump into in a medical emergency! It is used in surgery to drain away blood and prevent it from clotting during operations.

Books

Dawson, Ian. *Greek and Roman Medicine*. New York: Enchanted Lion Books, 2005.

Parker, Steve. *Groundbreakers: Alexander Fleming*. Chicago: Heinemann Library, 2001.

Sneddon, Robert. *Microlife: Scientists and Discoveries*. Chicago: Heinemann Library, 2000.

Using the Internet

Explore the Internet to find out more about **medicine** through the ages. You can use a search engine, such as www.yahooligans.com, and type in keywords such as:

- **bacteria**;
- **disinfectant**; and
- Alexander Fleming + **penicillin**.

Search tips

There are billions of pages on the Internet, so it can be difficult to find exactly what you are looking for.

These search tips will help you find useful websites more quickly:

- Know exactly what you want to find out about first.
- Use two to six keywords in a search, putting the most important words first.
- Be precise. Only use names of people, places, or things.

Glossary

Aborigine native Australian person

acne skin condition causing red spots, usually on the face

addicted find it difficult to get through the day without taking a particular drug

allergy unpleasant reaction to a substance

antibiotic substance that kills harmful bacteria

antidepressant drug to treat depression

antiseptic substance that stops harmful bacteria from growing and spreading disease

apothecary maker and keeper of drugs

arsenic white, powdery poison

asthma disease affecting the lungs that makes breathing difficult

athlete's foot itchy fungus infection between the toes

bacteria group of tiny living things. Some can cause disease.

bicarbonate of soda type of salt used to treat acid in the stomach

bowel part of the intestine where waste is held before it is let out of the body

caffeine drug found in coffee and tea

cell tiny building blocks that make up all living things

Christian follower of Jesus Christ and the religion based on his teachings

civil war when soldiers from the same country fight against one another

crucifixion put to death by being nailed to a wooden cross

depression feeling very down, upset, and deeply unhappy

diabetes disease in which the body is unable to use sugars in the way it needs for everyday function

diarrhea frequent loose or watery waste

digitalis drug used to treat the heart. It is made from the foxglove plant.

disabled having a physical or mental problem that can affect everyday life

disinfectant chemical that destroys germs

dose amount or measure of a medication or drug

edema illness causing fluid collection in the body. It often resulted in death.

epidemic outbreak of a disease that spreads quickly over a wide area

Epsom salts natural salts used as a laxative

eucalyptus Australian tree with oily leaves

excrement body waste

fever very high body temperature caused by illness

field hospital makeshift hospital, often in a tent near the battlefield

gangrene when flesh rots and dies due to infection or lack of blood supply

gout painful swelling of the toe

heart attack sudden failure of the heart

immune protected from catching a disease

infected carrying a disease-causing substance in your system

infection disease-causing substance that has taken hold in the body

ingredient something that goes into a mixture or recipe

inhaler device for breathing in a drug

insulin chemical made in the pancreas that controls sugar in the body

intestine part of the body that goes from the stomach to the anus. It is where food is digested.

Islam religion of Muslims, who follow the teaching of the prophet Muhammad

Islamic related to Islam

jaundice disease of the liver that makes the skin turn yellow

Kaposi's sarcoma cancer of the tissues beneath the surface of the skin

kidney stone hard lump that builds up in the kidney

laxative substance that makes you need to empty your bowels

leprosy disease that causes damage to the nerves and skin

licorice plant root that is used in many medications and in cooking

mandrake poisonous plant. The root was once used as a drug.

marrow soft, fatty jelly inside bones

medication substance used to treat illness or disease

medicine science of dealing with health and disease

Mediterranean Sea large sea south of Europe

Middle Ages period of history roughly between AD 500 and AD 1500

midwife nurse who helps women in childbirth

monastery place where monks live

monk member of a religious community of men

mortar pot in which material is pounded with a tool called a pestle

myth made-up tale that is told over the years and passed on

Native American member of any tribe of Indian in North America, South America, and the Arctic

nutrients important and healthy substances needed by the body

obesity being very overweight

ointment oily substance rubbed onto skin for medicinal reasons

opium drug made from opium poppies. It is used to help people relax and to relieve pain.

ovary female organ that produces eggs

pancreas organ near the stomach that controls sugar in the blood

penicillin first type of antibiotic

pharmacist person who prepares and gives medication

pharmacy shop where medication is prepared and sold

plague deadly disease that spreads quickly

pope head of the Catholic Church

potion liquid mixture that can be used as a medication or poison

poultice soft, heated bag or bandage put onto a sore

prescription drug medication given by a doctor

quinine drug that, among other things, reduces fever. It is found in a type of tree bark.

rectum opening from the bowel to the anus

remedy medication or treatment that is meant to make an illness better

resistant able to fight back

salve healing or soothing ointment

serotonin chemical in the brain that helps the "feel good" factor

smallpox disease causing blisters all over the body

stress feeling under too much pressure

stroke sudden illness caused by a blood clot in the brain

strychnine kind of poisonous powder

tobacco dried leaves of a plant used for smoking or chewing

tranquilizer drug to help calm and relax

tuberculosis disease that causes fever and lung failure

tumor unusual growth in the body

ulcer open sore. It is often full of pus.

urine liquid passed from the body. It is usually pale yellow.

vaccine medication to make the body defend itself against a disease

virus tiny living thing that breaks into the body's cells and can cause disease

Index